Revolutionizing Customer Service with Virtual Reality

Winning Strategies

Table of Contents

Chapter 1. Introduction

In the spectacular burst of technological innovation, Virtual Reality (VR) is no longer just a playground for gamers, but a powerful tool capable of revolutionizing sectors, particularly customer service. Welcome to our Special Report, "Revolutionizing Customer Service with Virtual Reality: Winning Strategies," that decodes this transformative trend with a balanced blend of comprehensible and compelling writing. Dive into a captivating journey through state-of-the-art examples, insightful discussions, and winning strategies gathered from across the globe. The essence of this report lies not only in predicting a VR-powered future for customer service but also in empowering your business to create it. Get ready to embrace this wave of change that could redefine customer experiences, firmly placing your business at the forefront of innovation. And remember, your journey towards revolutionizing your customer service starts here!

Chapter 2. The Dawn of Virtual Reality in Customer Service

The nascent phase of virtual reality (VR) was dominated by the perception of it as a tool conceived for the realm of gaming. This, however, has rapidly changed over the last decade, serving to invert the common misconception of VR as a technology burdened with narrow functionalities. In the recent past, the expansive possibilities of VR have begun to permeate various sectors, with one promising area being customer service.

2.1. The Resurgence of VR

Arguably, the year 2010 marked the resurgence of VR. Palmer Luckey, a young tech enthusiast, made a prototype of what would later become the Oculus Rift, a high-quality VR headset. Oculus's success garnered widespread attention, translating into a $2 billion acquisition by Facebook in 2014. From this point onward, the race to harness the potential of VR began, leading to the development of various VR devices such as Sony's PlayStation VR, HTC Vive, and Samsung Gear VR.

While the gaming and entertainment sectors were the immediate target, businesses quickly recognized that VR could also be harnessed to reimagine customer service. As businesses began investing in VR, a technological revolution quietly unfolded – a revolt led by VR against obsolete customer service methods.

2.2. The Advent of VR in Customer Service

The uniqueness of VR lies in its ability to create immersive, interactive, and multi-sensory experiences. This capacity began changing the customer service landscape as early as 2015. Some early adopters started providing virtual customer service in which customers could interact with virtual agents, receive instant responses, and have a personalized 'real-life-like' interaction.

This new trend was quickly validated by the numbers. According to a report from the International Data Corporation (IDC), spending on AR/VR products and services was expected to reach $27 billion by the end of 2018, and a significant proportion of this was anticipated to be spent in the realm of customer service.

Moving from experimentation to mainstream acceptance, several case studies highlighted the multiple applications of VR in customer service.

2.3. The Transformation of Retail

One of the early sectors to take advantage of VR was retail. Global brands like IKEA launched VR applications, allowing customers to experience their products in a virtual environment before making a purchase. These VR applications use 3D modeling to replicate every detail of a product, enabling customers to make informed decisions, reducing product returns, and therefore, minimizing the subsequent customer support.

Other retail businesses followed suit with VR 'try-on' experiences. Fashion and accessories brands, for instance, introduced VR fitting rooms that allow customers to try on clothes, shoes, and accessories virtually, bypassing the necessity for a physical trial. As a result, customers enjoyed a blended online-offline shopping experience that significantly reduced the need for a support service due to product dissatisfaction.

2.4. Impact on the Telecom Industry

The telecommunications sector also quickly found incredible value in leveraging VR technology. Companies like Verizon initiated the use of VR to train their customer service representatives (CSR). With the use of VR, CSRs could simulate various customer scenarios and practice their response. This VR-supported training led to better preparedness, equipping CSRs to handle a variety of customers and service situations, which ultimately resulted in improved customer satisfaction.

This new form of training also steered toward an eco-friendly approach, as the need for physical resources diminished, resulting in reduced carbon footprints, making it a win-win for all stakeholders.

2.5. Reimagining Customer Education

Beyond serving customers' immediate needs, VR also shifted the paradigm by enabling businesses to offer proactive support – primarily by educating customers about products or services using immersive experiences. Automotive companies, such as Audi and Ford, have used VR to demonstrate how their vehicles operate, allowing customers to virtually see each component and understand its respective function. This enriches the customers' knowledge about their purchase and reduces the likelihood of product misuse, thereby reducing the volume of customer service tickets associated with user problems.

2.6. Redefining After-sales Service

The impact of VR extended to after-sales service as well. Companies like Coca-Cola used VR to assist vending machine owners with maintaining their machines. By wearing a VR headset, an owner could see step-by-step visual instructions guiding them on how to service the machine. This not only provided a 'self-service' solution for machine owners but also freed up Coca-Cola's customer service resources for other support services.

This transformation is reshaping not just the expectations of customers who can now essentially become their own service providers but also the resources businesses allocate to customer service, with an overall positive impact on efficiency.

2.7. Influencing the Travel and Tourism Sector

Travel and tourism were not far behind in integrating VR into customer service. Companies like Marriott used VR to allow hotel visitors to tour rooms and facilities before even setting foot on the premises. Sharing virtual tours of holiday destinations, airlines like Lufthansa provided customers with a taste of the destination before actually booking their flights.

These immersive experiences serve as a selling point, enticing customers and minimizing disappointment post-booking, arising from unmet expectations. Hence, VR indirectly supports customer service by preemptively resolving customer issues.

In the short span of a decade, the dawn of virtual reality in customer service transformed from an idea into a reality. And with the promise that the technology holds, the future of customer service augmented by VR shines even brighter. As the world moves faster towards digitization, companies investing in VR today are the ones set to lead the customer service of tomorrow.

Chapter 3. The Technology Behind VR and Its Evolution

Virtual Reality (VR) has rapidly evolved from a mere futuristic concept to a ubiquitous tool in the realm of technology. It encourages us to examine what it is, how it works, and how it has transformed over time.

3.1. Understanding Virtual Reality

Virtual reality is a synthetic experience that can be comparable to or distinct from the real world. It manipulates a user's perception of reality via a system made up of an immersive interface and a rendering process to create a virtual environment. It uses specific technology to stimulate the user's senses and create the impression of being in a completely different environment.

Users are surrounded by artificial sensory stimuli such as sights, sounds, and sometimes smells and tastes, usually delivered via a headset. They can interact with the environment, which will react in response, creating a deeper sense of immersion. All these stimuli collectively blur the lines between physical and virtual reality and engage the user within a 3D computer-created simulation.

3.2. VR Technology: An In-depth Look

The heart of VR technology lies in the creation and rendering of the virtual environment and the delivery of this reality to the user.

1. **Display technology**: The primary task of VR display tech is to present users with a lifelike virtual environment. This is currently delivered through VR headsets such as the Oculus Rift,

HTC Vive, or PlayStation VR.

2. **Motion tracking**: The key to immersive VR experiences is motion tracking. As users move their heads or bodies, the VR system must adjust the view within the virtual world to reflect these movements.

3. **Graphics rendering**: The VR system needs to quickly and accurately render 3D graphics as users look around and interact with the virtual world. This requires powerful processing capabilities, either within the VR device itself or from an external source like a PC or game console.

4. **User interaction**: Finally, user interaction with the virtual world brings VR to life. This can take many forms, from handheld controllers to motion capture, voice recognition, eye tracking, and more.

3.3. The Evolution of VR: A Glimpse through Time

Although the consumer market has seen a surge in VR popularity over the past decade, the concept and development of VR dates back to the mid-20th century.

1. **Early VR concepts**: The first VR-like experience was Morton Heilig's "Sensorama" in the 1950s and 60s. It was a non-interactive theatre experience that could stimulate multiple senses, providing 3D images, stereo sound, vibrations, and even smells.

2. **Head-mounted displays**: Ivan Sutherland and his student Bob Sproull created the first VR headset, known as the "Sword of Damocles," in 1968. However, due to its enormous size and weight, it wasn't practical for user adoption.

3. **First commercial VR tech**: The 1980s and 90s gave rise to the first wave of commercial VR, with companies like VPL Research

and the Virtuality Group launching VR glasses and gloves. However, due to limitations in technology and high costs, the products didn't reach the mass market.

4. **Modern VR breakthroughs**: The game-changer appeared in 2010 when Palmer Luckey developed the first prototype of the Oculus Rift. This instigated the modern era of VR, defined by full immersion and user interaction, marking the concept's shift from the laboratory to the living room.

3.4. The Expanding Landscape of VR Applications

Over the past decade, VR has seen an explosion of innovation, translating into real, practical applications beyond video gaming. From virtual tours, training, simulation, therapy, to education, the dynamic landscape of VR applications continues to broaden, constantly pushing the boundaries of technology and creativity.

Indeed, the journey of VR from a scientific novelty to a household term underscores its definite potentiality. As technology progresses, so will the capabilities of VR, leading to more advanced, versatile, and immersive experiences in the future. We stand at the precipice of a technological revolution, defined in part by the achievements and future promises of Virtual Reality.

Chapter 4. Customer Service Before and After VR: A Comparative Analysis

Before the rise of Virtual Reality (VR), customer service often was viewed as a reactive function. A customer would encounter a problem, reach out to the company through phone, email, or social media, and a representative would attempt to resolve the issue. This model, while useful, was frequently cumbersome, time-consuming, and frustrating. It also lacked the flexibility and personalization that modern customers have come to expect.

4.1. The Traditional Customer Service Paradigm

The traditional customer service model primarily functioned on a complaint-resolution basis. Customers would contact the service organization after encountering a problem or having a question. While support teams made significant efforts to resolve issues quickly, the process often required extended interaction. The primary goal was to extract information from the customer about the issue, identify the cause, and then find a solution.

There were several disadvantages to this model. The heavy reliance on communication between the customer and the representative could lead to misunderstandings, and the resolution process was often lengthy and frustrating. Furthermore, it was difficult to personalize service because of the limited scope of customer interactions. Often, the engagement was purely transactional, lacking the human touch that customers seek.

4.2. Customer Service in the Digital Era: The Emergence of Online Platforms

As technology progressed, new platforms emerged that allowed for more direct interaction between customers and businesses. Email, for example, became an increasingly popular business communication tool. Social media channels proliferated, offering customers a public forum where they could express their concerns or appreciation.

At the same time, advancements in data analytics and AI brought about the potential for greater personalization. By tracking customer behaviors and preferences, companies could predict customer needs and offer a tailored service experience. Moreover, AI-driven chatbots enabled customer support 24/7, reducing wait time and improving customer engagement.

However, this digital transformation also led to an increased expectation for instant resolution and seamless customer experiences. It became clearer that companies needed to pivot from reactive to proactive customer service strategies.

4.3. Enter Virtual Reality: A New Paradigm for Customer Service

Paralleling these changes, the development and adoption of Virtual Reality (VR) began gaining momentum. Initially associated mainly with gaming and entertainment, this cutting-edge technology has shown potential to revolutionize various sectors, including customer service.

With VR, instead of relying on verbal or textual communication to understand a customer's problem, service agents can 'step into' the problem, gaining a more intuitive understanding. This capability dramatically reduces potential for misunderstanding between customers and service representatives, and it ultimately speeds up the problem-solving process.

4.4. Beyond Problem-Solving: An Immersive Customer Experience

But VR's impact on customer service goes beyond improving problem-solving. VR offers an immersive experience, providing an opportunity to showcase products or services in a unique, engaging way. Whether it is a virtual tour of a hotel room or a demo of a product virtually, VR has transgressed the physical limitations of traditional customer experience.

In this scenario, customers are not merely passive spectators, but active participants in the service ecosystem. By leveraging VR, businesses can deliver personalized experiences based on customer preferences. For example, a retail company could recreate a virtual store around a customer's shopping tastes, or a travel agency could offer a virtual tour of a holiday destination based on the client's preferences.

4.5. Personalization and Proactivity: The New Tenets of Customer Service

As VR technology becomes more widespread and sophisticated, its influence on the customer service sector will continue to grow. Customers will expect not just solutions to their problems, but also experiences tailored to their preferences. Moreover, businesses will increasingly need to adopt a proactive approach, predicting potential issues before they occur and preemptively offering solutions or alternatives.

In this context, Virtual Reality emerges not just as an innovative tool, but as a vehicle for a customer service revolution. Through its immersive nature and the potential for personalization and proactive service, VR is helping redefine customer experiences, positioning businesses on the vanguard of the digital revolution.

4.6. Seizing the VR Opportunity: A Strategy for Success

To take full advantage of VR's potential, companies should develop a comprehensive strategy that incorporates the various facets of this technology. This might include training customer service agents in VR, developing VR interactions that are intuitive and enjoyable, and employing sophisticated analytics to tailor VR experiences to individual customer preferences.

Investing in VR for customer service means more than just purchasing equipment and software. It also involves a deep culture change, from one that views customer service as a cost center to one that sees it as a potential source of customer satisfaction, loyalty, and even revenue.

To wrap up, the use of VR in customer service is not just about technology—it's about transforming the consumer-business relationship. It's about going beyond troubleshooting and service delivery to create memorable, customized, proactive, and immersive customer experiences. As such, it's a journey that every forward-thinking business should embark on to stay ahead in this competitive world.

Chapter 5. Case Studies: Successful VR Implementations

Even as discussions around Virtual Reality (VR) centered primarily on its overwhelming potential in gaming or entertainment, few foresaw its pivotal role in revolutionizing the way businesses offer customer services. However, across the globe, a handful of businesses have already started deploying VR in innovative ways to enhance customer service. Let's turn our attention to these ventures and the successful outcomes they've achieved through implementing VR technology.

5.1. Case Study 1: IKEA – Embracing VR to Simulate Experience

As a global leader in home furnishings, IKEA is known for its innovative approach to enhancing the purchasing experience. The Swedish giant leveraged VR technology to launch an immersive experience called IKEA VR Experience.

The novel platform allows IKEA customers to virtually experience a well-designed, fully furnished IKEA kitchen from the depth of a virtual environment. Users can explore different layouts, colors, and solutions, enhancing their informed decision-making process. The successful implementation of VR resulted in improved customer satisfaction and elevated sales, proving the efficacy of VR in retail customer service.

5.2. Case Study 2: Marriott Hotels - Teleporting Experience

When it comes to customer service, the hospitality industry, rightly or not, has always been held to an extraordinarily high standard. Marriott, the multinational hospitality company, rose brilliantly to this challenge through its innovative VR postcards.

Marriott's "VRoom Service" enables hotel guests to order in-room VR experiences, transporting them to compelling travel narratives in exotic locations such as Chile, Rwanda, and China, all from the comfort of their hotel room. This implementation not only enriched their customers' stay but also provided a unique preview of potential vacations, leading to a surge in room and travel bookings.

5.3. Case Study 3: British Gas – Enhancing Field Service Training with VR

Moving away from the retail and hospitality sector, the successful implementation of VR by British Gas, the UK's biggest energy provider, underscores its potential in servicing B2B customers.

By integrating VR into their field service training, British Gas enabled its engineers to practice complex installations, repairs, and maintenance routines in a safe, controlled environment. Technicians' proficiency significantly improved, leading to better customer service, fewer callbacks due to errors, and significant savings on service costs.

5.4. Case Study 4: Anthem – Leveraging VR in Healthcare

Anthem, a prominent US health insurance provider, successfully demonstrated VR's potential in the healthcare sector. They incorporated VR technology into their customer education program, compellingly presenting complex information on health conditions and treatment methods.

Customers found the virtual sessions far more engaging than conventional methods and showed enhanced understanding, leading to better healthcare decisions. Moreover, the sessions helped strengthen Anthem's partnership with its clientele, showcasing VR's role in fostering long-term customer relationships.

5.5. Case Study 5: Audi – Driving Experience Beyond Reality

In the automotive sector, the global brand Audi successfully employed VR technology to power its Audi VR Experience. This immersive platform enables customers to configuration their desired Audi model in an immersive virtual environment.

From virtually sitting in the car, feeling the interior, and experiencing the drive, each detail is designed to mimic reality. This not only transforms the pre-purchase experience for customers but also assists them in making more informed decisions. The resulting surge in customer engagement and higher conversion rates reflect the significant impact that VR can have on automotive branding and customer service.

As each of these case studies demonstrates, VR has the potential to add a new dimension to customer service and experience. Whether it's retail, healthcare, hospitality, energy, or automotive, VR's ability to create immersive, engaging experiences can help businesses revolutionize their customer service, enhance their brand image, and drive growth. What's clear is that the stories of these VR pioneers will surely inspire more businesses to explore and unleash the limitless potential of VR to redefine their customer service.

Chapter 6. Step-by-Step Guide: How to Apply VR in Your Customer Service

In the transformative galaxy of technology, where Artificial Intelligence (AI), Internet of Things (IoT), and other marvels continue to dazzle, Virtual Reality (VR) stands tall as a formidable pioneer. A robust tool with immense potential, its application in various sectors, most notably customer service, is impressive, and complex. This step-by-step guide highlights the 'how' of applying VR in your customer service.

6.1. Understand the Basics and Potential of VR

Before planning to incorporate VR into your business model, it is imperative to understand the technology deeply. Virtual Reality is an immersive technology that transports users to different environments, be it real or imagined, recreated digitally. It can be used to simulate a physical presence in the real world or an imagined environment, thus making it an effective tool to enhance customer interactions.

From conducting product demonstrations, offering immersive customer support, to giving users a hands-on experience of your offerings, VR holds tremendous potential for customer service. It can create immediate, engaging, and meaningful experiences for customers, thereby promoting customer satisfaction and loyalty.

6.2. Identify Your Needs and Define Goals

Begin by identifying the needs of your business and customers. Do you need VR to enhance product demonstrations, provide effective customer support, or deliver immersive training to your customer service staff? Once you have identified the need, define your goals. Clear objectives can serve as the foundation of your VR strategy while providing a benchmark for measuring its effectiveness.

Consider discussing with stakeholders, including employees and customers. Their feedback, coupled with data from customer service analytics, can provide valuable insights into areas of your customer service that can significantly benefit from VR integration.

6.3. Choose the Right VR Solution

VR solutions vary in cost, complexity, and capabilities. From smartphone-powered experiences that use VR apps and headsets, to high-end solutions that require powerful processing hardware, there are a plethora of options available. The choice of VR solution depends on your budget, needs, and the level of immersion you want to provide.

For instance, low-cost solutions can be used for virtual customer support and basic product demonstrations. High-end solutions, on the other hand, are ideal for delivering interactive and highly immersive experiences, such as virtual product trials.

Consult with a VR solutions provider or a technology consultant to identify the best VR solution that meets your needs and fits your budget.

6.4. Develop Your VR Content

After choosing the right VR solution, focus on creating compelling VR content that would be engaging and helpful for your customers. Make sure your content is interactive and easy-to-navigate.

Remember, effective VR content is not just about stunning visuals; it's about creating a complete immersive experience. This means considering all aspects, including graphics, sound, and user interaction. For instance, if you are using VR for product demonstrations, the user must be able to easily view, manipulate, and interact with the product in a virtual environment.

6.5. Train Your Staff

Before you can reap the benefits of VR in customer service, your team needs to be comfortable using the technology. Provide comprehensive training to your customer service staff, covering everything from using the VR hardware and software, to handling customer queries in a virtual environment.

Investing in regular training and upskilling can help ensure your team leverages the full potential of VR technology, leading to enhanced customer satisfaction.

6.6. Test and Implement the VR Solution

Once your staff is trained, begin the testing phase. Testing helps identify any potential issues or areas of improvement before a full-scale implementation. As testing progresses and issues are addressed, you can gradually roll out the VR solution to your customers.

Always request customer feedback on your new VR offerings. This will provide you with essential insights that can help refine your approach, making it more user-friendly and appealing over time.

6.7. Evaluate and Optimize

After implementing your VR solution, regularly evaluate its performance using Key Performance Indicators (KPIs) including customer satisfaction, reduced resolution time, or increased sales.

Optimization should be an ongoing process based on regular evaluations. Leverage customer feedback, analytics data, and staff inputs to constantly refine your VR strategy.

The integration of VR offers profound versatility that can transform the way you deliver customer service. This guide illuminates the path towards reaping the unparalleled benefits of this innovative technology. As you embark on this journey, remember to keep your customers' needs central. After all, superior customer service begins and ends with the customer. Your pursuit towards VR-powered customer service is your commitment to delivering unforgettable experiences - an ethos that always propels businesses towards sublime success.

Chapter 7. Winning Strategies for VR Integration in Customer Service

Implementing technology such as Virtual Reality (VR) into your customer service model requires well-crafted strategies. With VR, the possibilities of enhancing customer service interactions are endless. From improving the overall customer experience to offering real-time solutions, the advantages are remarkable.

7.1. Understanding VR and Its Scope

To devise a winning strategy, you first need to completely understand what VR is and its potential. VR is a computer-generated simulation in which a person can interact within an artificial 3D environment using electronic devices, such as VR goggles, helmet-mounted displays, or gloves fitted with sensors. The scope of VR extends beyond enhancing gaming experiences and has impressive potential in sectors like healthcare, education, and most notably, customer service.

7.2. Identifying Goals and Setting Key Performance Indicators (KPIs)

A clear identification of what your organization seeks to achieve with VR is crucial for creating an effective strategy. Goals could vary from business to business, but mostly revolve around improving customer satisfaction levels, reducing service time, or providing immersive product demonstrations. KPIs must be set to measure the success or lack thereof for the implementation of VR. Common KPIs for VR could be customer satisfaction scores, average issue resolution time, or Net Promoter Score (NPS).

7.3. Evaluating Business Needs and Customer Expectations

Gain insights into what your customers want; consider their expectations, preferences, and pain points. Researching and gathering data through surveys or feedback can be beneficial. Adopting a customer-centric approach when integrating VR into your customer service operations will result in improved customer satisfaction and increased customer loyalty.

7.4. Adoption of a Phased Approach

Instead of a complete overhaul of your current systems, adoption of a phased approach towards VR integration can be more beneficial. Start with one aspect of customer service, gauge its efficiency, then progressively expand to other areas. This allows for better risk management and gives ample scope for refinements.

7.5. Training Teams to Manage VR Tools

Once you've decided to leverage VR, your staff needs to be trained accordingly. Remember, success does not solely depend on technology, but also rests on how well your team can use that technology to meet customer needs. An investment in staff training ensures a smooth transition to VR while minimizing downtime and maintaining high standards of customer service.

7.6. Investment in Robust VR Software and Hardware

Choosing suitable VR hardware and software is key to the successful integration of VR into your customer service strategy. Ensure that the software is compatible with current systems and capable of handling future upgrades. The hardware, too, must be high quality and capable of providing an engaging and immersive VR experience for your customers.

7.7. Regular Monitoring and Ongoing Improvement

After the successful integration of VR into your business operations, regular monitoring is essential to identify bottlenecks and challenges. With constant improvement and updates, your VR strategies will keep pace with the ongoing technological advances and evolving customer expectations.

In conclusion, winning strategies for VR integration in customer service are driven by a comprehensive understanding of VR, clear goal setting, a phased approach to implementation, consistent team training, investment in robust VR hardware and software, and a commitment to regular monitoring and improvement. With these strategies, businesses can leverage the potential of VR to revolutionize their customer service and outshine their competitors.

By integrating VR into your customer service approach strategically and decisively, you can foster an environment dedicated to enhanced customer satisfaction. This is the point where technology and human efforts meet to create a unique and immersive customer experience. Indeed, your journey towards revolutionizing customer service with VR starts here. Achieving futuristic customer services isn't so far fetched; it's just a matter of making the right strategic choices.

Chapter 8. Overcoming Challenges of VR Adoption in Customer Service

Technology adoption, despite its numerous advantages, is rarely a linear or smooth process. Among disruptive technologies, Virtual Reality (VR) sets a bright example. It has an unlimited potential to revolutionize the customer service industry by improving user interaction, fostering better understanding, and enhancing communication. However, a question that remains is: Are companies and customers adequately equipped to embrace this transformative technology? These challenges, ranging from financial constraints to the readiness of infrastructure, need due consideration for an effective VR implementation.

8.1. Financial Constraints

Indisputably, cost stands as one of the most significant challenges in VR integration into customer service operations. High-quality VR equipment is costly, and investing in it requires businesses to balance the upfront costs against the potential long-term benefits, which can be nebulous at the beginning.

Establishing a cutting-edge VR-enabled customer service setting not only involves purchasing VR headsets but also requires investing in allied technologies, including advanced software, high-speed internet, and maintenance facilities. The continuous development in VR technology also implies the inevitable hardware upgrades that come with a considerable expense.

Therefore, companies should begin by assessing their financial capability against the cost of VR adoption. A step-wise adoption, starting with specific customer service areas where VR can provide considerable advantages, might be a pragmatic approach.

8.2. Technological Readiness

The successful implementation of VR technology requires a robust technical infrastructure. The demand for high-speed internet connectivity to support real-time VR interactions can be a significant hurdle. Insufficient bandwidth or high latency could result in low quality VR experiences, potentially frustrating customers and hampering the productivity of customer service representatives.

Similarly, companies must ensure the compatibility of their existing systems and software with the emerging VR technology. Scrutinizing whether or not their current technological stack can adapt and integrate with VR is decisive.

On the other side, customers also need to possess the necessary hardware and software to receive VR-enabled customer service. Not all customers, especially in developing regions, will have access to a VR-ready environment. Companies need to consider their customer demographics carefully and gradually introduce VR as one of many channels for customer service.

8.3. Human Factor Challenges

Adopting new technology, especially something as revolutionary as VR, often faces resistance from both employees and customers due to unfamiliarity or perceived complexities.

For employees, training to use VR technology efficiently can be demanding. It goes beyond understanding the technology – they also need to be acquainted with new ways of communication and problem-solving in the VR world. Thus, developing a comprehensive training program for employees is essential to make this transition smooth. The program should aim at enriching their skills and creating an environment supportive of change.

From a customer's perspective, comfort and ease of use are critical. Any technological malfunction or difficulty in use can lead to customer frustration and potentially damage the relationship. Therefore, customer education on VR usage should complement company initiatives towards VR adoption.

8.4. Data Security Concerns

Given the immersive nature of VR, the data involved can be highly sensitive. Companies will potentially hold personal information, behavior patterns, and even biometric data of customers. Hence, data privacy and security become paramount. Businesses need to strictly abide by data protection laws and reassure their customers that their data is safe and used responsibly.

8.5. Regulatory Landscape

The rapid advancement of technology always brings about new regulatory challenges. Currently, VR technology's regulations are still in the nascent stages, which leaves room for potential confusion and risk. Businesses must navigate these uncertainties and ensure their practices align with any existing or forthcoming regulations.

In conclusion, while VR's potential in customer service is immense, businesses need to carefully traverse through these challenges. A considered approach which embraces the merits of VR and simultaneously addresses the challenges could arm companies with this powerful customer service tool, setting them apart in the competitive landscape.

Chapter 9. Future Trends: How VR Will Shape Customer Experiences

Ever since its inception, Virtual Reality (VR) has created ripples of interest, capturing imaginations and releasing a wave of potentialities. Immersed in a sense of wonder, users can explore virtual spaces, interact with elements, and experience environments with a perceived level of reality. The immersive traits of VR make it ideal for customer service, offering unique ways to engage customers, meet their needs more effectively, and create unmatched experiences.

9.1. VR: The Key to an Immersive Customer Experience

The potential of VR as a powerful tool in crafting immersive customer experiences is immense. It's not just about providing service; it's about inviting customers into an innovative realm where every interaction is handcrafted to their needs. Thanks to VR, businesses can now distill the essence of their service and translate it into a rich, immersive experience.

VR provides a sense of presence unparalleled by any medium to date. When customers use VR, they are engaged on a multi-sensory level, providing a deeper connection to the brand than what's achievable through traditional channels. This immersive nature leads to memorable experiences, making a much more significant impression on the customer's psyche.

9.2. Transforming E-commerce with VR

The E-commerce industry stands to benefit hugely from the adoption of VR technologies. Imagine shopping for a living room sofa and being able to visualize exactly how each model would look in your own home. VR not only allows customers to get realistic previews of products in situ, but it also enables them to experience the item in unique ways which a 2D photo will never capture, fostering confidence during their purchase journey.

Brands can harness VR to offer virtual showrooms where customers can explore products in hyper-realistic 3D, walk around them, interact, and even customize for a personalized touch. These actions go way beyond basic 'product view' and offer customers a more enriched, satisfactory shopping experience.

More advanced applications use mixed reality, combining VR with augmented reality (AR) to offer real-time customization. Customers can visualize products in their premises with their unique specifications, generating a powerful sense of ownership before purchase.

9.3. Revolutionizing the Travel & Hospitality Industry

VR is also emerging as a powerful tool in the travel and hospitality industry, where experiential service is pivotal. Through the use of VR, potential tourists can experience different travel destinations and offerings before deciding on their itineraries. This use of VR offers an unprecedented method of marketing, pulling customers in with tantalizing samples of experiences on offer.

Hotels are leveraging VR to provide virtual tours of their facilities.

This goes a long way in fostering rapport with potential guests and establishing trust, as they can sample facilities and services before securing a booking.

VR also provides an excellent platform for training in the hospitality industry. Employees can acclimate to hands-on job requirements in a real-world setting, making the learning process safer, more effective, and engaging.

9.4. Improvement in Education and Training

Customer support plays a crucial role in industries such as software or equipment manufacturing, where new users need training. Deploying VR can help customers understand and effectively use new products without needing to attend physical training sessions.

Companies can create 3D virtual environments of their software, where the customer can engage and manipulate features in real-time. For physical products, companies can simulate disassembly and re-assembly of an appliance, guiding users on how to maintain or repair their devices.

9.5. VR in Healthcare Customer Service

In healthcare, VR has shown promise in patient care as a tool for therapy and pain management. However, its potential extends further into customer service, improving how healthcare professionals engage with patients.

For instance, VR could allow patients to navigate 3D representations of their medical data, such as MRI scans, in company with their doctors, creating dynamic discussions about treatment plans. It could also be used for remote consultations, where both parties interact in a virtual space, breaking barriers of distance and mobility.

9.6. The Infusion of AI with VR

Artificial Intelligence (AI) and VR together can achieve synergistic effects in customer service. Businesses can leverage AI's prowess in pattern recognition and decision-making with VR's immersive customer experiences.

Imagine a virtual store where an AI assistant interacts with customers, guiding, recommending based on past purchase history, and even upselling or cross-selling products. Combining these technologies opens up opportunities for personalized customer service on a degree currently unattainable.

9.7. Dealing with the Challenges of VR

As with any other technology, VR adoption in customer service has challenges. Setting up a VR infrastructure requires significant investment in hardware and software development – a drawback for smaller enterprises. Additionally, creating efficient VR content requires specialized skills, pushing up project costs.

Furthermore, there's the issue of standards and compatibility. As VR hasn't fully matured, there are many competing technologies and formats, complicating the effort of creating content deployable across various platforms.

9.8. Looking Ahead

Given its potential, it is eerily exciting to contemplate how VR will shape the future of customer service. As technologies advance, costs reduce, and standardized solutions emerge, we will likely witness a rapid uptake of VR across sectors. Still, the onus remains on businesses to understand how VR can integrate with their operations and how to harness its potential to enrich the customer experience.

VR is not just a technology; it's a whole new language for customer experience. The future will see VR becoming more than a tool – it will become a standard, a medium through which customers engage with services. Businesses that recognize this trend and adapt may be the ones to secure customer loyalty in the future.

This exploration into the future trends of VR in customer service paints a thrilling picture of unprecedented experiences and paths to customer satisfaction yet to be tread. While there might be challenges to conquer, the opportunity to redefine the landscape of customer service with VR appears more than promising. After all, in the race towards customer satisfaction, the most exciting part is not just reaching the destination but the journey of innovation.

Chapter 10. Measuring the Impact of VR on Customer Satisfaction

Understanding this chapter's task necessitates that we first address the concept of customer satisfaction. Traditionally, customer satisfaction has been gauged through feedback and surveys, direct interactions with clients, ratings and reviews, and social media sentiment analysis. While these methods have been effective, they are all post-consumption measures. The cutting-edge capability of VR offers the possibility to measure customer satisfaction during the service encounter itself, in real time, providing more accurate and valuable insights.

10.1. The Essence of Real-Time Customer Feedback

One of the most significant benefits provided by the implementation of VR is the possibility of collecting instantaneous customer feedback. Unlike traditional methods, VR tracks and records user interactions while they are experiencing the service. This provides an unfiltered, real-time representation of their experiences and reveals insights into their likes, dislikes, areas of interest, and overall engagement. For example, VR platforms can collect data on where and on what the customer's gaze lingers longest, or which interactive elements they engage with the most. These details can be instrumental in determining customer satisfaction and can help in innovatively refining service offerings.

10.2. Exploring VR Metrics for Customer Satisfaction

To measure the impact of VR on customer satisfaction, we need to establish relevant metrics. Here are some key ones to consider:

1. Emotion Recognition: With advanced AI, VR can analyze users' facial expressions and vocal cues to detect their emotional state during the service encounter. This instant feedback could be a substantial game-changer in gauging customer satisfaction.

2. User Engagement Metrics: By tracking user interactions, VR can accurately gauge engagement. Time spent on certain sections of the VR experience, frequency of interactions, or areas where users seem to get stuck, are all potential indicators of satisfaction or dissatisfaction.

3. Heatmaps: These color-coded graphical representations of data can track the frequency of gaze and interaction with different sectors of the VR environment. Hotter areas on the heatmap have more activity, providing a quick visual representation of customer preferences.

4. Physiological Responses: Advanced VR technologies can measure physiological responses such as heart rate and skin conductivity to gather data on user arousal and excitement.

10.3. The Power of Predictive Analytics

Once metrics are established and data is collected, Predictive Analytics can help extract valuable insights from the data and influence future decision-making. It uses statistical models and forecasts to predict future outcomes, providing actionable insights into what clients want before they even ask for it. This can facilitate proactive modifications of VR experiences to maximize customer satisfaction.

Predictive Analytics can identify behavioral patterns and emerging trends by synthesizing data from multiple sources, including VR experiences, social media sentiment, purchasing habits, and previous customer feedback.

10.4. Implementing Changes for Enhanced Customer Satisfaction

Data collection and analysis are just the beginning. The real value lies in using insights to refine and enhance VR experiences. By understanding user preferences, companies can personalize VR environments to better address individual needs and wants. This adaptability can significantly improve customer satisfaction and loyalty.

Additionally, customer satisfaction measurement can be gamified within a VR environment. Encouraging customers to rate or rank their experiences within the VR system prompts instant feedback and demonstrates commitment to customer satisfaction.

10.5. Customer Satisfaction, The Ultimate Business Goal

While VR's potential to revolutionize customer service is immense, the end goal should always be enhancing customer satisfaction. Virtual Reality is a tool that, when used right, can provide a deeper understanding of your customers' needs, wants and expectations.

We wrap up this exhaustive chapter on "Measuring the Impact of VR on Customer Satisfaction" by highlighting that as VR evolves, so should the techniques for tracking, measuring and enhancing customer satisfaction. Investing in VR technology is not just about keeping up with trends, but also about re-defining your relationship with your customer in a rapidly changing digital landscape. Truth be told, in this incredibly competitive business environment, the companies that put the customer at the core by consistently nurturing and refining their satisfaction, are the ones that shine. Remember, your tech investments are a means to an end, the customer should always be the ultimate goal.

Chapter 11. Preparing for a VR-Driven Customer Service Future

Cyberspace has transformed businesses in numerous ways, and the customer service landscape is no different. We stand at the precipice of another digital revolution, one that will take customer service into the realm of Virtual Reality (VR). VR technology presents service representatives and customers alike with an immersive and interactive medium that elevates the quality and efficiency of service interactions, transcending geographical limitations.

11.1. Understanding Virtual Reality

Virtual Reality signifies a three-dimensional, computer-created environment that can be interacted with by individuals. This technology engrosses users by simulating as many senses as possible, such as vision, hearing, touch, and even smell. The subjectivity of this experience is what sets VR apart from traditional user interfaces.

A comprehensive understanding of VR technology is essential for businesses planning to incorporate it into their customer service. Three main types of VR technology currently coexist: non-immersive, semi-immersive, and fully immersive. Non-immersive VR is the least engaging form, typically used for video gaming. Semi-immersive VR offers a more interactive experience, typically used for simulations. Finally, fully immersive VR offers users the most realistic and interactive experience. Markedly, the level of engagement directly correlates with the necessary equipment and cost.

11.2. The Need for VR in Customer Service

Customer expectations have seen a paradigm shift due to the rampant digitization and personalization in service industries. Traditional modes of customer service including emails, phone calls, or face-to-face communication often fail to deliver the level of personalization that modern customers seek.

Moreover, language barriers and cultural differences often pose challenges in delivering exceptional customer service. With the help of advanced VR technologies, businesses can transcend these barriers and provide superior, immersive experiences to their customers, thereby leading to higher satisfaction and loyalty.

11.3. Implementing VR: Getting Started

To begin with, businesses considering the VR leap must conduct a thorough assessment of their current customer service performance. This strategic audit should highlight the existing service gaps, customer preferences, and areas of improvement. At the same time, realizing the potential advantages and constraints of VR is critical.

Upon this foundation, an implementation plan can be drafted. This includes identifying key performance indicators (KPIs) for the VR-driven customer service, defining the scope of the VR initiative (fully immersive, semi-immersive, or non-immersive), and setting a realistic timeline for the launch.

11.4. Overcoming Implementation Hurdles

The integration of VR technology into existing customer service infrastructure can present significant challenges. These range from finding the right hardware and software to training the customer service team effectively. In addition, the potential digital divide among customers - differential accessibility to and familiarity with VR technology – requires careful consideration.

Furthermore, data security is a paramount concern when dealing with VR tech. As personal data is further exposed within the VR environment, businesses need to prioritize the establishment of robust data management and protection strategies.

11.5. Training and Skill Acquisition

A key aspect of facilitating the VR transition is providing ample training to the customer service representatives. Becoming adept at using the VR equipment and software, and leveraging these to enhance customer interactions, will require dedicated training sessions. These sessions must target both the technical competencies and soft skills required to deliver top-notch VR customer service.

11.6. Future of VR in Customer Services

Looking towards the horizon, businesses will continue to innovate with VR, making it a central component of their customer service strategy. The capacity of VR to create unique, personalized, and highly engaging customer experiences positions it at the forefront of the service industry's future. This transformation is poised to extend VR's influence beyond customer service, into areas such as product development and marketing.

By recognizing and embracing these disruptions now, companies can significantly enhance their competitiveness in the rapidly evolving market landscape. This will place organizations that exploit these opportunities at the helm of the customer service revolution.

In conclusion, VR represents a powerful tool to elevate customer service. Its depth and flexibility give it the potential to transcend traditional boundaries and bring about enhanced customer satisfaction. Investing in VR technology now will not just be an upgrade—it is the future. Businesses need to understand this—and be ready to embrace it.